THE EXPECTATION MINDSET:

Understanding and Utilizing the Impacts of Expectations

By Noah Foster

Table of contents

Preface

The Expectation Effect: Understanding and Utilizing the Impacts of Expectations explores the profound influence that expectations may have on our lives. The term "expectation effect" describes a phenomenon in which our expectations affect our reality and can affect how things turn out when we do certain actions. The purpose of this book is to examine the science of expectations, the influence of optimistic expectations, and methods for dealing with unfavorable expectations.

Research has shown that expectations can significantly affect our behavior, emotions, and general well-being. The subject of expectations has been extensively studied in the fields of psychology and neuroscience. Expectations may affect how we see and interpret information, how motivated and engaged we are, and even how our bodies react physically.

The expectation impact may be observed in a variety of facets of life, including our close relationships, professional goals, physical well-being, and financial achievement. In contrast, those with negative expectations may underperform or fail to land the opportunity. As an illustration, people with positive expectations for a job interview may be more likely to perform well and land the job. Similarly to this, people who have optimistic expectations for their health may take better care of themselves and have better health outcomes, whereas others who have pessimistic expectations may ignore their health and have chronic health problems more frequently.

This book will examine the science of expectations and how they affect the world around us. We'll also look at the influence of optimistic expectations and how they might improve a variety of life outcomes. We'll go through ways to deal with unfavorable expectations as well as case studies of people and organizations who have used expectations to their advantage.

The Expectation Effect is a potent instrument that can alter both our lives and the society we live in. We may use the power of our expectations to improve both our own lives and the lives of people around us by comprehending the science underlying expectations, cultivating a positive mentality, and taking action to dispel unfavorable expectations.

In summary, this book explains how our expectations shape our reality and can influence the outcome of our actions. The book also aims to provide readers with strategies to develop a positive mindset, overcome negative expectations, and harness the power of expectations to create a better reality for themselves and those around them.

Chapter One: Introduction

The term "expectations" in the context of the expectation effect refers to our assumptions or mental representations of what is likely to occur in a certain circumstance. These expectations, which might affect our perceptions, emotions, and conduct in that circumstance, can be derived from prior experiences, social standards, or personal objectives and aspirations. The term "expectation effect" describes a phenomenon in which our expectations affect how we feel and even how things turn out. This could take the shape of self-fulfilling prophesies, in which our actions cause our expectations to materialize.

Many different kinds of expectations might affect how we see the world and how we experience it. Some examples include:

1. Self-imposed expectations

These are the hopes and objectives we establish for ourselves. They might be simple or huge goals that relate to either career or personal success.

2. Societal expectations

These are the customs and practices that are accepted within a certain culture or society. They can include, among other things, expectations about gender roles, educational accomplishments, and professional success.

3. Other's expectations

These are the standards we have for the conduct and deeds of others. They could relate to what we anticipate from friends, family, or coworkers, and they might affect how we engage with them.

4. Implicit expectations

These are the beliefs or previous experiences-based expectations that we retain implicitly. Without our knowledge, they can affect the way we think and act.

5. Explicit expectations

These are the expectations that we can name and are aware of. They can be impacted by our objectives, ideas, and emotions, and they might be connected to a particular event or circumstance.

It's important to keep in mind that various kinds of expectations can overlap, interact, and have both favorable and unfavorable consequences on our perceptions and experiences.

Shaping Reality Through Expectations

Our ability to receive and understand information is influenced by our expectations, which can then affect how we see reality. When we have preconceived notions, we frequently pay more attention to data that supports those notions and less attention to data that does not. Confirmation bias is a phenomenon where people deliberately seek out and analyze data in a way that confirms their preconceptions. This can result from certain circumstances.

Additionally, the information that matches our expectations is more likely to be encoded and recalled, while the information that doesn't match our expectations is more likely to be forgotten. Overall, our expectations can have a big impact on how we see and understand the world.

Our reality is built on the basis of our beliefs. They shape our thoughts, emotions, and actions, and ultimately determine the way we perceive the world around us. In this chapter, we will explore the concept of beliefs and how they shape our reality. We will look at the different types of beliefs, the role they play in our lives, and the impact they have on our well-being.

Types of Beliefs

Beliefs may be classified into several distinct categories, including self-beliefs, beliefs about other people, and worldviews. The beliefs we have about ourselves, such as our capacities, value, and potential, are known as self-beliefs. The views we have about the individuals in our lives, including their capabilities, intentions, and motives, are known as beliefs about others. The worldviews we have regarding natural laws, the nature of reality, and the proper order of things are examples of worldviews.

The Role of Beliefs

Our world is greatly influenced by our beliefs. They have an impact on our perception of the world around us by influencing our ideas, emotions, and behaviors. Our self-esteem, self-worth, and confidence, for instance, might be impacted by the views we have about ourselves. Our interactions with others and our relationships can be impacted by our beliefs about other individuals. The way we perceive the world and how we interpret experiences and events may both be influenced by our worldviews.

The Impact of Beliefs

Our well-being is significantly impacted by our beliefs. Negative thoughts can result in failure, dissatisfaction, and ill mental and physical health, whereas positive beliefs can increase success, happiness, and general well-being. For instance, we are more likely to establish and accomplish our objectives if we feel capable and deserving of success. On the other side, we are less likely to establish and accomplish our objectives if we feel unworthy or incapable, which can result in emotions of failure and inadequacy.

Confirmation Bias

A cognitive bias known as confirmation bias makes us look for and interpret information in a way that supports our prior ideas. Even when confronted with fresh or contradictory evidence, this might make it challenging for us to question and revise our ideas. It's critical to be aware of this prejudice and make an effort to seek out different ideas and consider them.

Challenging and Changing Limiting Beliefs

Limiting beliefs are unfavorable assumptions that keep us from moving forward and accomplishing our objectives. Examining the evidence for and against these limiting ideas will help you identify them and fight them. We may start the process of modifying our limiting beliefs after we've discovered them by swapping them out for more powerful and positive ones.

ChapterTwo: The Science of Expectations

The study of expectations spans a variety of academic fields, including psychology, neuroscience, and social science. It is a complicated and multifaceted field. Our expectations can significantly affect our behavior, emotions, and general well-being, according to research in this field.

The idea of the self-fulfilling prophecy is a crucial component in the science of expectations. This is a reference to the phenomena wherein our expectations might affect how something turns out. For instance, if a person is confident and performs well at a job interview, they may increase their chances of getting the job. On the other side, if someone is expecting to do poorly at an interview, they could perform poorly out of nervousness, which would reduce their chances of landing the job.

The significance of cognitive biases is another crucial facet of expectations science. Several cognitive biases might affect our expectations, including the halo effect and confirmation bias. The term "confirmation bias" describes the propensity to look for and interpret information in a way that supports our preexisting views and expectations. The propensity to judge a person's overall worth based on only one quality or attribute is known as the "halo effect." For instance, even though there is no proof to back it, someone may believe that a job applicant would fit well into the business culture if they have high expectations for them based on their impressive résumé.

Additionally, studies have demonstrated that our expectations might affect how our bodies react. People who have high expectations for a task, for instance, could feel less stressed and more satisfied than others who have low expectations, who can feel more stressed and less satisfied.

Current research has shed light on some of the ways that expectations affect our behavior and emotions, however, the psychological and neurological mechanisms behind expectations are still being explored and understood.

From a psychological standpoint, expectations can affect how we see and interpret data. For instance, we could be more likely to notice and interpret information positively if we have optimistic expectations for a circumstance. On the other side, if we anticipate something going wrong, we could be more likely to pay attention to and see information negatively.

Expectations may also affect how motivated and engaged we are. Others who have optimistic expectations about a task may be more driven and involved in it, whereas people who have pessimistic expectations may be less so.

From a neurological standpoint, expectations can affect how the brain functions in specific areas. For instance, studies have revealed that when people have high expectations for a task, their prefrontal cortex activity, which is involved in decision-making and attention, increases. The amygdala, a part of the brain involved in emotional processing, also exhibits increased activity when people have unfavorable expectations for a task, according to a study.

Overall, there are numerous, intricate, and complicated psychological and neurological processes that underlie expectations. Expectations can affect how we see and interpret information, how motivated and engaged we are, and how much specific brain areas are active. To completely comprehend the workings of expectations and how they affect our behavior and emotions, more research is required.

In conclusion, many different disciplines make up the vast and comprehensive area of expectations science. According to research, our expectations may significantly affect how we behave, feel, and how happy we are as a whole. Expectations have the power to alter our physiological reactions, cognitive biases, and event outcomes. To fully appreciate expectations' influence on our lives and learn how to use them to our advantage, it is essential to comprehend the science underlying them.

Chapter Three: The Power of Positive Expectations

Positive expectations are the conviction that favorable events will occur in the future. Positive expectations can help our behavior, emotions, and general well-being in a variety of ways, according to research. Positive expectations may boost motivation and engagement, which is one of their main advantages. People are more likely to be involved in the process and more driven to strive toward goals when they have good expectations regarding a task or scenario. Better performance and more favorable results may result from this elevated drive and involvement.

Additionally, having optimistic aspirations might help our mental health. Positive expectations often lead to reduced levels of stress and higher levels of enjoyment, which can improve mental health. Additionally, having optimistic expectations can encourage feelings of hope and optimism, which can improve a person's attitude toward life in general.

Positive expectations can provide better results in terms of certain life areas including relationships, careers, health, and financial success.

- In terms of relationships, those with high aspirations frequently have more solid and satisfying partnerships. They could be more inclined to resolve problems amicably and to see their interpersonal interactions favorably. This may result in improved contentment and closer relationships with others.

- Positive expectations can result in improved job performance and increased success in accomplishing professional goals. Positive expectations increase motivation and engagement at work, which can improve performance and open up more career progression prospects for those who hold them. Positive expectations may also make people more willing to take measured risks and take advantage of chances that might increase their chances of success.

- Positive expectations can result in improved health results in terms of health. People who have high expectations for their health are more likely to take care of themselves and practice healthy habits like frequent exercise and a balanced diet. Better physical, mental, and emotional health and well-being may result from this.

- Positive expectations can result in improved financial planning and decision-making in terms of success financially. Positive expectations tend to increase optimism and decrease concern about the future of their finances, which can improve financial planning and decision-making. Greater financial stability and prosperity may result from this.

Positive expectations may often result in better results in a variety of life areas, including relationships, jobs, health, and financial success. People are more likely to achieve their objectives and have meaningful and profitable lives if they cultivate a positive mentality and tackle problems with a constructive attitude.

Strategies for developing positive expectations

The development of optimistic expectations can be facilitated by several tactics. These comprise:

1. Setting prudent objectives

People may direct their energy and focus on what they want to accomplish by setting clear, defined, and attainable objectives. Setting realistic goals can assist people in breaking down challenging objectives into more achievable, smaller-scale tasks that are easier to complete.

2. Changing the way you view things

We may be less able to see possibilities and form constructive expectations if we have negative attitudes and beliefs. Reframing negative thinking entails recognizing and questioning negative attitudes and thoughts while substituting more uplifting and helpful ones. People may become more optimistic about life as a result of this.

3. Gratefulness exercises

By cultivating thankfulness, people may change their perspective from concentrating on what they lack to appreciating what they do have. People may cultivate a more upbeat mindset by constantly taking the time to acknowledge the wonderful things in their lives.

4. Mindfulness

Being present in the moment, which is the act of mindfulness, can assist people in keeping their attention on the here and now rather than worrying about the past or the future. Due to their freedom from negative feelings or ideas, people may find it easier to form good expectations.

5. Affirmations of success

Affirmations that assist people to change their thinking are brief, straightforward phrases that they may repeat to themselves. The phrases "I am competent," "I choose to be joyful," and "I trust in the result" are some examples.

6. Encircling yourself with constructive individuals

Our perspective and expectations might be significantly influenced by the individuals we spend the most time with. We may cultivate a more optimistic mindset and more readily accomplish our goals by surrounding ourselves with good, encouraging individuals.

By employing these techniques, people may cultivate optimistic expectations, which can result in improved outcomes in a variety of spheres of life. It is crucial to keep in mind that change does not occur instantly, but with perseverance and consistency, people may cultivate good expectations that will result in a happier and more affluent existence.

Significance of self-awareness and introspection in developing optimistic aspirations

Positivity expectations are created by self-awareness and self-reflection, which are essential components. They assist people in seeing the effects of their expectations on their lives and in identifying and comprehending their thoughts, feelings, and behaviors.

The capacity to identify one's thoughts, feelings, and behaviors in the here and now is known as self-awareness. People may then consciously choose how they wish to think, feel, and act by being aware of their own biases and habits. People can recognize their negative thinking patterns and beliefs, which may be impeding their capacity to form constructive expectations.

Thinking about and evaluating one's ideas, feelings, and behaviors is the process of self-reflection. It enables people to develop an understanding of how their expectations affect their life and to spot patterns and conduct that may be impeding them. Self-reflection can assist people in recognizing the areas of their lives where they could have unfavorable expectations and in creating plans to deal with them.

Self-awareness and self-reflection work together to help people realize how their expectations affect their life and cultivate a more upbeat outlook. People can become more conscious of their own biases and tendencies by becoming more aware of their thoughts and feelings. They can also choose their thoughts, feelings, and behaviors more consciously. Greater self-awareness and self-reflection may result from this, which may then encourage people to form optimistic expectations, which may ultimately provide better results in many aspects of life.

In conclusion, it is impossible to overestimate the value of self-awareness and self-reflection in developing optimistic expectations. These techniques assist people in understanding how expectations affect their life and in cultivating a more upbeat outlook. People can become more aware of their own biases and tendencies by practicing self-awareness and self-reflection. They can also choose their thoughts more consciously.

Case studies of people and businesses that have successfully used optimistic expectations to further their objectives

- Bill Gates is a prime example of how having high expectations can result in success. Bill Gates is the co-founder of Microsoft. Gates had a distinct idea of what he wanted to accomplish from an early age, and he continually set both ambitious and reasonable objectives for himself. He had high hopes for starting and growing a great computer software firm, and he succeeded in doing so via perseverance and hard work. His optimistic outlook resulted in the founding of one of the most prosperous businesses in the world as well as his financial success.

- The media magnate and philanthropist Oprah Winfrey are another illustrations of how having high expectations may result in success. Winfrey has continuously maintained high expectations for herself and has established high standards for herself. She has achieved success in her career as a talk show host, an actress, and an entrepreneur. She has also used her success to change the world for the better through philanthropy.

- Tony Robbins is a self-help author and motivational speaker who has successfully used the power of optimistic expectations to accomplish his objectives. Robbins continuously sets high standards for himself and has a good anticipation of assisting others in improving their life. His optimistic outlook has inspired the creation of effective personal development courses and seminars, and he has assisted thousands of individuals in realizing their ambitions.

- Malala Yousafzai, a supporter of girls' education and recipient of the Nobel Peace Prize, is a prime example of how having high expectations may result in achievement. Malala maintained an optimistic outlook on reaching her objective of ensuring that all girls had access to school despite overcoming several difficulties and impediments. She developed into a strong education champion as a result of her high expectations, and she has contributed to enhancing girls' access to school.

It's crucial to remember that, even though these people have succeeded greatly, success won't come to everyone easily. However, readers can increase their chances of success by maintaining a positive attitude, setting goals, and working toward them. Additionally, keep in mind that each person's journey is unique and that what works for one person may not work for another. Nevertheless, readers can find the approaches that work best for them by being open to various viewpoints and learning from the experiences of others.

Chapter Four: Overcoming Negative Expectations

Our lives might be significantly impacted by negative assumptions. They can harm our relationships and hinder our ability to accomplish our goals. They can also cause feelings of anxiety, depression, and hopelessness. Negative expectations can also cause us to unintentionally act in ways that cause those expectations to come true, which is known as a self-fulfilling prophecy. It may be beneficial to confront negative expectations and make an effort to recast them in a more positive perspective, practice mindfulness and encouraging self-talk, and seek assistance from loved ones, friends, or a therapist to lessen their negative effects.

Improving our life requires recognizing and dealing with negative expectations. Positive outlooks and the capacity to identify possibilities are both hampered by pessimistic expectations, which can have a detrimental effect on our behavior, emotions, and general well-being.

How to Recognize Negative Expectations

Finding them is one of the first stages in overcoming negative expectations. Due to strongly established and sometimes unconscious negative expectations, this can be a difficult undertaking. Here are some techniques to help you recognize your unfavorable expectations:

1. Reflect on your feelings and thoughts

Throughout the day, take some time to consider your feelings and thoughts. Pay attention to any persistently unpleasant thoughts and feelings. These could be a sign of unfavorable expectations. For instance, if you regularly experience feelings of helplessness or overwhelm, it may indicate that you have low expectations for your capacity to deal with particular circumstances or accomplish particular objectives.

2. Maintain a journal

Record your feelings and ideas in a journal. This might assist you in noticing trends and recurring themes in your unfavorable feelings and thoughts. You may keep track of how your expectations related to certain circumstances or occurrences by doing this.

3. Seek criticism

Find out what your close friends, family members, or a therapist think about your ideas and feelings. They might be able to identify any unspoken unfavorable expectations on your part. They could also be able to provide a distinct viewpoint on a circumstance that enables you to examine things from a fresh angle.

4. Contest presumptions

Examine your presumptions and views more carefully. Do you have any presumptions or views that are unfavorable or restricting? Do you, for instance, think that you will constantly fail or that you are not good enough? These unfavorable thoughts may prevent you from reaching your objectives and may be reducing your potential. You may gain a more optimistic perspective on things by challenging these ideas.

    5. Determine the origin of any unfavorable expectations.

It's critical to comprehend the source of your unfavorable expectations when you've discovered them. They could be the result of previous encounters, peer pressure, or even self-doubt. You can deal with these negative expectations more successfully if you know where they came from. For instance, you might need to go through your prior experiences in therapy if your negative expectations are the result of them. You might need to question societal standards and expectations if they are the result of pressure from the community.

You may better grasp how negative expectations are influencing your thoughts, emotions, and behavior by recognizing them. You may use this information to your advantage to get rid of these unfavorable expectations and replace them with fresh, constructive ones.

Additionally, it's critical to remember that detecting negative expectations is a continuous process because not all of them may be immediately apparent and others may be strongly embedded in our subconscious. It's crucial to be persistent and patient while locating and treating them.

Challenging Negative Expectations

The next stage is to question your unfavorable expectations when you've discovered them. This is a crucial step in overcoming unfavorable expectations and forming fresh, optimistic ones.

Here are some methods to help you confront unfavorable assumptions:

1. Contest the expectation's veracity

Examine the arguments in favor of and against the unfavorable hypothesis. Is it founded on truth or conjecture? Does the anticipation conflict with any evidence? You might start to perceive the expectation from a more realistic perspective by challenging its legitimacy.

2. Determine the direst situation.

Consider the worst-case scenario that may occur in the circumstance. Is it as horrible as you anticipate? Negative expectations frequently stem from anxiety and overstating the likelihood of a bad occurrence.

3. Look for success stories

Look for instances of people who, despite comparable unfavorable circumstances, managed to achieve. This might assist you to change your viewpoint and show that bad expectation isn't a given.

4. Rephrase the demand

Consider what might go right rather than what might go wrong. Changing your perspective and boosting your drive may be accomplished by positively reframing the expectation.

5. Get assistance

To assist you to confront unfavorable expectations, enlist the aid of close friends, relatives, or a therapist. They may give support and encouragement as well as a different point of view.

Negative expectations are difficult to overcome, and it could take some time before you notice a shift in your attitude. However, you may start to break free from the negative cycle and accomplish your goals by challenging the validity of negative expectations, identifying the worst-case scenario, seeking good examples, reframing expectations, and gaining assistance.

Developing Positive Self-Talk

Developing positive self-talk is a critical tactic for overcoming unfavorable expectations. The internal conversations we conduct with ourselves are referred to as self-talk, and they may have a big influence on our ideas, feelings, and behaviors. While good self-talk can help us change our perspective and boost our motivation, negative self-talk can perpetuate negative expectations. Here are some methods to develop positive self-talk:

1. Recognize negative self-talk

Becoming aware of the self-talk that is supporting your negative expectations can help you stop it. Examples of common ones are "I can't do it," "I'm not good enough," and "I'll never succeed." To change negative self-talk, you must first recognize it.

2. Engage in constructive self-talk.

When you've discovered negative self-talk, confront it by asking whether it's grounded in reality or just an assumption. Is there any proof to support positive self-talk? You may put the self-talk in a more realistic perspective by challenging it.

3. Use uplifting affirmations instead of critical self-talk.

Find encouraging statements to use in place of limiting thoughts. If you tell yourself, "I can't do it," for instance, a positive affirmation may be, "I am capable and have the potential to achieve." Regularly repeat these mantras to yourself, especially when you're feeling depressed or uninspired.

4. Demonstrate gratitude

Concentrate on the aspects of your life for which you are thankful. This can assist in helping you identify the positive parts of your life and divert your attention from negative self-talk and expectations. Additionally, it helps boost good feelings and lessen tension.

In conclusion, it is possible to have a satisfying life with the correct skills and mentality even if overcoming negative expectations is a process. We may escape the negative cycle and accomplish our goals by realizing the effects of negative expectations, tracing their origin, questioning them, cultivating positive self-talk, and getting help.

Chapter Five: The Impacts of Expectations on Decision-Making and Problem-Solving

Understanding how expectations and decision-making overlap

Expectations have a significant impact on how we see the environment and behave. They have the power to affect how we feel, think, and behave in a variety of circumstances. Our capacity for problem-solving and decision-making can both be impacted by our expectations. Expectations have the power to alter how we perceive the world and can serve as a lens through which we view it.

Expectations are the mental picture we have of the results we hope to achieve; they can be either good or negative. Positive expectations are the conviction that a specific outcome will materialize, whereas negative expectations are the conviction that a specific outcome won't. Expectations may come from inside or may be shaped by outside forces including past events, societal conventions, and cultural influences.

Expectations can significantly affect our capacity for problem-solving and decision-making. Positive expectations can foster greater innovation and creativity, but negative expectations might result in a more constrained and ineffective strategy. Our capacity to handle stress and uncertainty as well as our ability to see possibilities in challenging circumstances may both be enhanced by having positive expectations. On the other side, negative expectations can cause us to feel hopeless, powerless, and unmotivated, which can make it challenging to accomplish our objectives and lead a satisfying life.

This chapter will examine how expectations affect our ability to reason and solve problems as well as the connection between expectations and decision-making. We'll look at how expectations affect decision-making, both good and bad, as well as how to control expectations while making decisions and coming up with solutions to problems. Understanding the connection between expectations and decision-making can help us harness the power of optimistic expectations to enhance our capacity for problem-solving and decision-making.

Expectations may have both a good and a negative impact on cognitive functions and problem-solving. Positivity may improve cognitive functions and problem-solving skills by:

- Boosting motivation and involvement makes people more inclined to participate in problem-solving activities

- Enhancing focus and concentration to enable people to pay closer attention to pertinent information

- By providing fresh opportunities and viewpoints, expanding creativity and innovation

- Increasing the likelihood that people would retain pertinent information, hence improving memory and recall.

On the other side, unfavorable expectations might impair thinking and problem-solving skills by:

- A decline in interest and motivation that makes people less inclined to engage in problem-solving activities

- Reducing mental clarity and concentration by making people more aware of their unpleasant emotions and ideas

- Limiting innovation and creativity by eliminating options and viewpoints

- Reducing people's likelihood of recalling important information, which reduces memory and recall.

By affecting how we see and interpret information, expectations can also have an impact on our capacity to process and comprehend data. Positive expectations can increase our propensity to interpret information positively, whereas negative expectations can increase our propensity to interpret information negatively.

Expectations may also have an impact on how we approach problem-solving. Positive expectations can boost our openness to consider new possibilities and take chances, whereas negative expectations might increase our propensity to stick with tried-and-true methods and minimize risk-taking.

Overall, our cognitive functions and problem-solving skills can be significantly impacted by our expectations. While unfavorable expectations might hinder certain skills, positive expectations can help them. We may learn to harness the power of optimistic expectations to enhance our capacity for problem-solving and decision-making by comprehending how expectations affect cognitive functions and problem-solving.

The contribution of optimistic expectations to the promotion of innovation and creativity

Positive expectations play a crucial part in encouraging people to be innovative and creative. Positive expectations can aid people in cultivating an open-minded, inquisitive mentality, which is necessary for creativity and invention. Positive expectations lead people to focus more on chances and potential than restrictions and constraints. They may become more adventurous and receptive to different viewpoints as a result.

Positive expectations may encourage people to feel more motivated and engaged, which can inspire them to be more inventive and creative. People are more inclined to spend time and effort coming up with fresh ideas when they are motivated and interested. Additionally, they are more inclined to keep going in the face of challenges and bounce back fast from failures.

Additionally, having optimistic expectations might result in increased focus and concentration, which are crucial for invention and creativity. Positive expectations encourage people to pay attention to pertinent information and come up with fresh ideas. This may inspire people to create fresh and distinctive solutions to issues.

Positive expectations can also aid in the growth of a person's feeling of self-efficacy, which is crucial for invention and creativity. The conviction in one's capacity to succeed in a certain activity or circumstance is referred to as self-efficacy. People who feel highly in their abilities are more inclined to embark on difficult projects, persevere in the face of challenges, and bounce back fast from failures. They may come up with novel and creative solutions as a result.

In conclusion, optimistic expectations play a crucial part in encouraging people to be creative and innovative. A more open and inquisitive mentality, higher motivation and engagement, better attention and concentration, and a sense of self-efficacy may all be developed by people with positive expectations. People may empower themselves to come up with fresh concepts and answers, as well as to go over challenges and constraints, by cultivating optimistic expectations. As a result, people may achieve more achievement and personal growth, and workplaces may become more effective and productive.